Dare to Care
Reflections on the Art of Caring

Cheryl Masson

authorHOUSE®

AuthorHouse™
1663 Liberty Drive, Suite 200
Bloomington, IN 47403
www.authorhouse.com
Phone: 1-800-839-8640

First published by AuthorHouse 6/16/2009

ISBN: 978-1-4389-2444-1 (sc)

Printed in the United States of America
Bloomington, Indiana

This book is printed on acid-free paper.

Contents

Introduction

The concept of caring is a familiar-sounding one and yet it is somewhat elusive to most. The majority of people believe they are caring individuals. I myself have been a nurse for many years. As a health-care professional in a vocation that is known for its caregivers, I should have a complete understanding of caring concepts. Yet I spent years without really understanding the reality of a caring heart.

My misunderstanding began with believing that having a caring heart is a natural process. I believed that some of us are blessed with it; some of us are not. I also believed that those who are not blessed with a naturally caring heart experienced difficulty working in a service industry such as nursing. That was a great misconception.

<u>Dare to Care</u> is a practical look into the art of caring. The concept of caring is an expression of who we are in this great world. It also expresses what role we share in our interactions with others.

It actually says, "You matter to me." Caring creates possibilities for coping because we partner with those we know to discover new directions and provide motivation to grow. This is the essence of a caring heart.

Caring is relational. It is not just about performing tasks, but it is a willingness to enter into a relationship of understanding others' experiences (1), In 1991, Kristen Swanson developed a "theory of caring" which helped to develop useful and effective strategies to help the health-care community express caring. The main steps in the caring process are knowing, being, doing, enabling, and maintaining the other person. In utilizing these basic steps, we set up a foundation for effective partnerships of coping.

We expect that those people that are employed in the health-care field are experienced and fluent in the art of care giving. Unfortunately when caring aspects are missing in the nursing process, it creates a great void in our health-care system. The personal concern of a caring heart should be an inherent feature of the nursing profession. Unfortunately there is a lack of caring in many of the health-care institutions today.

I have been involved in nursing for many years. I educate young workers who are joining the nursing profession as entry-level employees. As these new staff members begin to actually step out into clinical practice, they begin to experience hands-on care giving. There were times that some of their clinical experiences did not go as well as we would expect. I have come to the understanding that caring is not something that comes naturally and instinctively. It is a concept that needs to be taught. I also have come to recognize the fact that health-care personnel are not the only professionals that need to learn the concepts of caring. I have a passion to see caring concepts taught on a personal level as well as a professional level to anyone willing to listen.

It certainly seems harder for some people to instinctively express a caring heart toward others. Some of my students were not able to naturally flow with the spirit of caring. My job was to educate all my students. It was still my job to teach even those students who did not seem to have a caring heart. I had to teach them to be caring professionals. So I decided to put together a curriculum to teach my students the basic steps of learning to care. If they could not do it on their own, then I was determined to train them to be caring.

The text of this book, Dare to Care, was compiled after my painstakingly trying to express my caring heart to the heart of all readers of this work. This book is a simple conversation piece from my heart to yours. It is my attempt to look at the issues that surround care giving in the nursing profession, a profession that was built on displaying the concepts of caring for others.

So I began teaching the curriculum that I had compiled for my students. When asking these students about the concepts of caring, I realized that everyone truly believes that they care and they believe that they know what it means to care. But when confronted with the question to describe what caring means, most people have a hard time articulating what caring is actually all about.

The purpose of this simple book is to break down the concepts of caring for all to examine. My hope is to help everyone to retake a look at these issues. I have learned in my life that sometimes issues become familiar and they begin to be taken for granted. The understanding of simple ideas tends to get clouded by the passage of time and by our lack of attention.

The time has come to revisit our thoughts concerning caring concepts. We need to examine our attitudes that affect the other people who share the space of our lives. By simply reviewing these elemental concepts, they will again become fresh in our minds and we will be able to exercise the caring heart that is within all of us. Dare to Care is a challenge to all of us. It is not only a challenge for those in caring professions, but to those in all walks of life. It is a challenge to hone these skills and begin to successfully practice them again. I ask that you take my dare and begin to care.

When we engage in relationships on any level, we find that we run into barriers to caring. Dare to

Care gives understanding of why people shy away from caring. As we learn about the concepts of caring, we will more easily and willingly embrace a heart of caring for those things that we are passionate about. Then we will seek out ways to express these new attitudes. Dare to Care gives guidance and practical direction to reach out and express those passions.

Caring is a concept that everyone who engages in any kind of relationship should understand and put into practice. It is at the core of every personal interaction. The art of caring is at everyone's disposal if we only dare to care.

Chapter 1
Why Do We Care?

From the beginning of time, human beings have had social interactions with others. They then had to effectively deal with the issues that arose from these social contacts. In the Bible, we see these issues crop up in the first story of Adam in the Garden of Eden. In the very beginning Adam had everything that God had created at his disposal. His life was wonderful, right? Not so. The Bible story tells us that God looked down at Adam and saw that it was not good. Adam was alone. He had at his disposal a wonderful garden where all his physical needs were met. He had every living thing in the garden with him, yet he was still alone. He needed human socialization. God then creates Eve to be a companion for Adam to complete him. In this story, this was the first social interaction, and it was good.

This first social interaction was a good one. Unfortunately, all interactions that came after that did not always culminate with a happy ending. Throughout history we see that on an individual basis as well as with group dynamics, sometimes our attempts to have good social interactions do not always succeed. They sometimes result in failure.

The human race is inclined by nature to need companionship with others. It is instinctual. We have an innate need to form cooperative or interdependent relationships with others. We usually gravitate to those who think and believe like we do. We like it when others are like-minded as we are and therefore are a reflection of ourselves. It reinforces our choices and our expectations and expresses that we are a part of something positive.

It is a fact of nature that we are social beings needing social interaction. The minute we are born, we join our first social group. That group is the family. From the moment of our birth, we begin social interactions: good and bad. No matter what the outcome of these interactions may be, they are inevitable.

Over time social mentalities about others as well as our actions toward others have gone through many changes. We can look back through history and see different societies have developed their own particular social norms and acceptable behaviors toward others. Some of these norms proved to be useful and we see them withstand the test of time. Others, however, have proved to be unacceptable to emerging societies and have gone by the wayside.

We find these changes to be true in our society today. As we move into the twenty-first century, our culture is going through many changes. Our cultural norms are no longer reminiscent of our elders' of the twentieth century. We can no longer make assumptions about other people's beliefs or value systems. The human race now has to have a global view of societal norms due to the fast-paced, transient society in which we live today. The so-called norms are no longer normal anymore.

There are some basic knowledge sets that have remained steadfast through time and that we still hold true in this day and age. These are the philosophical assumptions that we still believe today. They have been with us since the beginning of time. These assumptions hold true for each of us when we hold the "individual person" as the central focus of our values and beliefs. Let's look at these truths that have stood the test of time.

The first philosophic assumption is that every individual person is responsible for making decisions that influence their own lives. This is the right of self-determination. We also assume that each person is holistic. By this we mean that their physical, thinking, and feeling processes function together in a unified expression of their behavior patterns. We are three-part beings of mind, body, and spirit.

A second philosophical assumption is that we as people function interdependently with other people in environments to create societies (2). We are social beings. It is this final assumption that allows a caring spirit to grow and flourish. It is from this societal need that we find caring as an entity of our lives.

> *Caring says "you matter to me" and if you matter to me, then I will choose to do something for you.*

Individuals were not created to be alone. We were designed to be social beings. It is difficult at best to function without support or help from others. It is that connectedness with others that brings out the caring spirit from within us. Caring says "you matter to me" and if you matter to me, then I will choose to do something for you. Caring is an outflow of our personal selves because of the personal interest or affection we feel toward someone else.

Humans have genuine concern and regard for others. It is only a natural flow of human nature. That is a noble thing. Caring is not effective though, unless we reach outside of ourselves and take actions about those concerns that arise from within us concerning those things around us. We need to actually do something to touch the needs or problems of those around us. Caring is the action that we take to actually effect change in someone else's life. Caring is a word that demonstrates action. People should be a conduit for blessings to flow through them to others. Caring is not simply a mental or emotional exercise that is done mentally whenever we see our fellow humans in need. Thinking about a problem is not effective without taking some action to make a difference. Caring is an action word. Caring is the natural outflow of action which demonstrates my reaction to a situation of concern.

It is important that everyone understand what it means to care. Most people use the word but do not really understand the ramifications or the depths of its meaning. Before people can be expected to actually function in a caring mode, they must understand what it really means to care

Chapter 2
What Does It Mean To Care?

Caring is a word that is multifaceted. It has as its basic definition, connotations of worry, anxiety, and concern. These are considered negative emotions for some. People tend to shy away from things that cause them anxiety or worry. Most people do not want to experience emotions that tug on their heart. It hurts sometimes and they do not like the effect it can have on their emotions. It is this self-guardedness that keeps us from being effective in our relationships with others.

One prevailing thought of health and wellness reflects that health is a state of complete physical, mental, and social well-being (3). This thought is really limiting. Health is not the freedom from the inevitable disease, death, unhappiness, or stress that we experience in our daily lives. Health is the ability to cope with these inevitable changes in a competent and positive way (4).

Society today wants to alleviate all of our problems. The thought is to protect ourselves from problems and then we will not have to deal with them. The absence of stressors is not realistic. There is a saying that expresses it quite plainly: "Life happens." It happens around us every day. There are positive and negative occurrences and we need to know how to react and deal with both. Our euphoric attitudes want to protect us from anything that is not good and pleasant. We want all of our experiences to be positive ones. That attitude sets us up for failure and disappointment at the very least. It is through these times of adversity that we need to draw strength and support from others that surround us and are a part of our lives. Know this to be true—adverse times will arise for us or those that we love. It is through these times that we need to support one another with care.

How can we then go about giving care and being a caring person? There are realms of caring that we can use to touch others' lives. There is a physical realm and an emotional realm. Let's take a look at each of them.

The Physical Realm of Caring

When we set out to define what caring is, we can notice that there are two separate realms of existence. The first realm of caring is in the physical plane. Whether it is the giver or the recipient of the care, it is going to be experienced in the physical realm.

The first experience with care for everyone on earth began as they came out of their mother's womb. Infants require complete and constant care for their every need. Human caring is a universal phenomenon (5). Caring acts are necessary from the moment of our birth. They are also necessary for development and growth and human survival. These caring acts then eventually culminate to and are necessary to assist with everyone's peaceful death.

Our physical bodies have five basic needs to survive. They are oxygenation, nutrition, elimination, activity, and rest (6). Our functioning and our survival depend on these needs being met. The hierarchy of needs set up by the behaviorist Maslow, show that the basic physical needs of a human being must be met before their emotional and esteem issues even arise in the human experience (7).

To care for someone in the physical realm means to reach out and touch others to meet their physical needs. There are professions that have been developed on the premise of meeting people's physical needs. But again, to meet anyone's needs, it takes physical action. We have to do something. Caring requires action.

Caring requires action.

The avenues that can be used to show physical caring may be varied and different, but they all revolve around the aspect of action. In the case of the infant or a small child, it involves the physical care, protection, and nurturing of that child. Put into the realm of an individual with an illness, it means physical care, protection, and education. When we are thinking of the individuals who are lacking the five basic needs in their lives that it takes to survive, it means providing those things that are essential to survival.

Physical care is not limited to an individual connection—a one-on-one interaction. It can also be a societal connection between groups of people. This kind of caring is on a larger scope than just a one-on-one, individual basis. It does not matter, however, how large the scope is. It still requires action to be effective. The effectiveness of caring depends on the fact that we as individuals or as corporate groups let the caring flow through us and effectively touch others with our actions. I see caring as a conduit of blessing. Conduits are defined as channels through which water or other fluids are transported. Conduits are likened to fountains flowing freely. That is how I see a caring heart. It is an open pipeline that carries the ability to reach out and touch an issue of need. But again it takes action.

The Emotional Realm of Caring

Caring for others on the emotional level can be the hardest process for most people because this realm causes us distress and personal pain. Caring on an emotional level causes us grief. When we experience suffering in our minds, it gives us a burdensome sense of responsibility towards the needs that we see.

Caring creates concern in our minds. Concern brings a troubled state of mind because we are personally interested or relationally involved and thus are compelled to the situation. Not only do we not want to experience the emotional tugging that comes with this realm of caring, but we also have a hard time with reaching out and connecting with others on this level. This is a great contrast to the euphoric state we desire to live in. We want our lives to run smoothly—no problems, no troubles.

People do not want to experience the struggle of caring because it can be personally painful in some way. People are also reluctant to express emotions to others or in public. Most people do not know how to respond to heartaches and tears. Being around others that are shedding tears makes people uncomfortable. It is the first response of most people to see that the crying stops. We say, "Stop crying, it will be okay"; whether it is true or not is not our concern. We just want the crying to stop. This response is out of preserving personal well-being instead of being focused on the heartache that we are encountering.

It is hard to know how to respond to someone who is brokenhearted. A very common response is to walk away in self-protection. I have seen it many times in my personal life and in my professional walk. Most people do not mean to be heartless but they do not know what to say or how to act. They do not want to take on the heartache so they retreat and run away.

Many times in my health-care career I have been in situations of heartache. There are many caregivers who are in the trenches, working with the sick and dying. They are also given the task of caring for the family members who are heartbroken over their sick loved ones. These caregivers have confided to me that they were ashamed of the fact that they would cry and feel the emotions in these tough situations. My encouragement to them is that crying only shows that they are human. It is not a character flaw to be touched with concern and then to reach out and touch a hurting person with emotional kindness and caring. It is in our human character to care.

I had a personal experience with a neighbor who did not know how to react to my personal bad situation. The area where I lived had experienced a tornado. There was a lot of physical damage to our home and property. I was thankful that my family remained safe through the ordeal. After the bad weather had passed, the neighbors came out to survey the damage in the area. I was standing in the backyard looking at the back of the house. The tornado had blown out windows and a tree limb had fallen and was sticking out of the roof. The rain had soaked the inside of the back half of my home. It was a mess. As I was surveying the damage and the totality of the damage was sinking in, I began to feel the crushing weight of my loss. At that moment my neighbor approached me. As she began talking about the damaged house, I began to cry. She had a pivotal moment. She could have embraced me and supported me with encouraging words or she could have even cried with me. She did not. She stated to me, "Don't you be crying," and she walked away.

The price of caring is the personal giving of ourselves.

Unfortunately this is a typical reaction to emotionally stressful situations. People will turn and run away instead of standing and dealing with the emotional stress. They are reluctant to share in others' emotional stress. It simply is a reaction of self-preservation. Wrong as it may be, they shrink away from the situation. That is unfortunate for both parties. They then wonder why no one is there to support them in their time of need. Emotional caring is taxing and causes us to give emotionally of ourselves. This tugging on our heart strings is the aspect of caring that our society must learn to embrace and cultivate again. This struggle is the problem most people have with caring. There is a cost when it comes to caring and most people are reluctant to pay the price. The price of caring is the personal giving of ourselves.

Chapter 3
The Cost Of Caring

The act of caring is not without cost. Caring in itself is a mentality of action from one person to another. It causes someone to reach out with a purpose to help the other in need. Caring is an action word. Not always extensive but always intending to effect a change for the better in the life of someone else.

The act of caring begins in the heart and then in the mind. A need must be recognized before a response can be offered. Facilitating empathy for others is the steppingstone to action. To have empathy for someone else shows the ability to understand the experience the other person is facing without losing yourself in their situation. It is the ability to comprehend another person's point of view. Having empathy is the ability to perceive accurately other persons' feelings and being able to convey their meaning with understanding of that particular situation. Empathy allows us to be able to maintain our objectivity in the situation and yet be able to reach out and touch the other person right where they are.

There are some simple ways to facilitate empathy in any situation that we might find ourselves in. We need to sharpen our communication skills. First we must be an active listener. Being an active listener means that we must participate in the conversation. There is a significant difference between hearing and listening. Hearing is the physical functioning of the organ of the ear. The external ear catches sound waves, brings them into the ear canal, and the vibrations create sounds. At this point we hear different sounds. But listening involves using your brain to understand these sounds. Listening also involves assimilating the information and paying attention to what you hear. That means we must pay attention to the message that is being conveyed. We also must be keenly aware of any behaviors being expressed. Nonverbal communication cannot be ignored.

Nonverbal communication is a form of communication that does not include words. The old adage is true; actions do speak louder than words. Researchers conclude that nonverbal cues carry approximately two-thirds of the communicative nature of a message (8). That is why it is imperative to be aware of nonverbal communication and that takes active listening; it is important to be aware that personal biases and preconceived ideas of judgment must be safeguarded against. Self-

> *In this day and age of global-mindedness we must not limit our scope to the boundaries of our own small existence.*

checks must be done periodically to thwart these tendencies. In this day and age of global-mindedness we must not limit our scope to the boundaries of our own small existence. We need to have the ability to embrace the differences and not be divided by them. Then we will be able to have a mental picture of the other person's situation and we must be open to embrace these differences.

Then it is imperative to think before you speak. Once you are communicating, you can then mirror the other person's energy and language. Be careful not to use clichés that are actually meaningless and at times offensive. You have to pay attention to the conversation to be able to mirror the other person's conversation. Finally and most importantly, you need to be authentic and genuine in your responses.

Already it is apparent that it is going to take effort to begin the process of caring by learning how to communicate effectively. This first step has already been taken by you. You began by just reading this chapter. One of the costs of caring is being paid right now by your time and attention to this information.

There is a cost physically and emotionally to caring. I want you to understand that the prize is worth the cost. That prize is to touch another individual's life. We have the opportunity to change lives one person at a time. One touch, one smile, one kind word, one moment to listen, one grasp of a hand can change the course of any situation. We are social beings, placed on this earth to interact with each other. Every single day, situations arise that put us in a position where we can effect change for someone. We can stop and give one act of kindness to just one person at any one moment. Do not underestimate the power you have at your disposal. That power is to touch and change the lives around you.

Giving of our time, our money, our hearts, and our lives does come with a price. That price is paid by self-denial. It hurts our flesh when we say no to ourselves. It is natural to protect ourselves. We want to let our flesh shy away and retreat from taxing situations. We want a euphoric life where everything is good—no troubles, no worries. But that is just not reality. In the world we live in, troubles do come. Our responses to these situations will determine the outcome for ourselves and those around us.

This is a great gift that is at our disposal. This gift is the ability to touch other people's lives and make a difference for them. This gift is within every one of us. There are certainly many situations that are placed before us daily that give us an opportunity to convey our caring and to share our gift. Yet for some reason there is a hesitation to express our care and concern. There is a mentality in the hearts of people that holds us back from the natural flow of this precious ability. There is something that wants to block that conduit of caring. We need to understand the mentality that restricts that flow.

What Holds Us Back?

There are two specific mentalities that restrict the act of caring among people today. I am not sure where this thinking came from, but I am sure I know why it exists and flourishes. People do not naturally flow with a caring spirit because of the personal cost that caring brings with it. It costs us either physically or spiritually and we are reluctant to give of ourselves. It is a self-centered mentality.

We are reluctant to give of ourselves because it has personal cost. When our mentality is based on the protection of ourselves, it does not seem right to do things that put a strain on our personal selves. Again, we have that misconception that our lives must have a euphoric existence—no problems, no troubles. When in reality we need to understand that a balanced life is dependent on our ability to accommodate to the problems that will definitely come our way. Our human ability for adaptation to the difficult life situations which will inevitably come our way creates the social hierarchies in which we live. Those people who have the ability to adapt well will persevere.

The ability to persevere is rooted in the survival of "self." A selfless attitude is not a balanced attitude either. There must be a balance of self-awareness and the awareness of others. It is when our focus becomes completely on ourselves that we get out of balance.

A self-centered attitude is a natural attitude. So do not feel condemned or guilty. We come into the world kicking and screaming to have our needs met. Just take a toy away from a toddler and see what kind of reaction you would get. It is all about self-preservation. However, when we grow and mature, we must learn to balance our own needs with the needs of others.

I did a word study on the word "self." I found that no matter what source I used there were pages of concepts that have a focus on self. Nearly every single thing we do can have a self-focus. The problem comes when we miss everyone else around us and we focus on ourselves.

Our understanding of self-focus usually encompasses those concepts of selfishness, being self-centered or self-absorbed. These concepts show a focus of helping one's self. We also need to be aware of the concepts like being self-critical, having self-abasement or self-denial are also self-absorbed concepts. These concepts may have a negative focus on "self" but they are still self-directed. Self-absorption is an insidious thing. It is subtle and it creeps up on us gradually and we are unaware of its effects. Most people are just living their lives, trying to make ends meet. They are just trying to meet their very basic needs. And again there is nothing wrong with taking care of you. The next thing you know, some problems will arise and you will be involved in taking care of your own issues to the extent that the needs of others are obliterated by the self-focus. Again you must balance your existence with caring for yourself, but still having a caring heart for others. And when that scale tips too far one way or the other, we are out of balance. It is a tightrope walk that we must master by constant awareness and attention to these issues.

The first thinking pattern that restricts us is the "I don't care" mentality. If we do not care, then we do not have to pay the price. This attitude of not caring will eventually reduce us to carelessness. Can we be so emotionally cold that our sense of caring has disappeared? But society today says it is okay not to care. It is okay to be detached emotionally from other people's situations. Some believe that other people's problems are not their business. We believe that their misfortunes should not affect us. Our thinking tells us that we have our own life and our own problems. Other people's problems do not encompass what is going on with me. Their misfortunes do not touch my life.

The sense of community is fading from our lives. We are detached physically and emotionally.

If we have no attachments we remain oblivious of anyone else's troubles. If we do not know what is wrong, our responsibility is null and void. We then have no accountability for others.

This "I don't care" mentality has got to change. We were created social beings with an innate need to interact with others. This mentality has forgotten the four essential philosophical assumptions thriving civilizations were built on. The first assumption tells us that every individual person is of value and is worthy of respect. The second tells us that each person is responsible to make decisions concerning themselves. We also assume that everyone is a thinking, feeling, and active person, and finally that we were created to interact one with another (9). We are social beings! We are community beings. Our lives are not complete when we have a solitary lifestyle. We were created to be caring individuals. An "I don't care" mentality does not fit in the natural flow of a society. This is an altered mentality within our society that must be addressed if we are to continue to thrive.

The other mentality that impedes the caring process is the "What about me?" philosophy. This mentality says, "I care," but mainly about myself. These people place the needs and desires of themselves as the priority for their decision making. They believe they are at the center of their world and everyone else revolves around them. If I were to open any sociology book or any book having to do with interpersonal skills, I would find a lot of information on "self." You will read about self-concept, self-actualization, self-awareness, self-care models, self-doubt, self-esteem, self-reflection, and I could go on. Our lives are inundated with information to focus on ourselves. One would have a difficult time finding information on developing a social conscience. Where is the information about service that is geared for others? It is something that is not focused on in our academic circles these days. Our teachings have been saturated with self-concept theories that are individually focused. It is time that the focus shifts from our inward man and begins to flow outward. This concept is the basis of caring. We let the blessings that come to us as individuals, flow through us to others. We must be conduits of blessings that flow freely. If we refuse to be a conduit then we become a reservoir that has only one direction. That direction is inward. A reservoir is a place that we keep an extra reserve. What happens when water sits in one place and does not flow? It becomes stagnant. The same thing happens in our lives when we become reservoirs for "things." Things flow into our lives. We keep them and hoard them and then they become stagnant. Then they become no use to us or anyone else. When we share these things with others, there will be a positive effect in their lives and ours.

This concept of being a conduit can be expressed

in the physical realm or in the emotional realm. A great example in the physical realm would be to take a look into your attics or basements or your garages. How many things do you have in your own homes that you do not use every day? How much is in there that you have not used or even seen in years? Just think about how those things could be utilized by someone else. Some of it might be put to good use. Some of it may not even be useful at all anymore. But by simply looking at this one issue we see that we are prone to being a reservoir. I am sure that you will be able to come up with many other examples once you start giving it some thought. I picture this ability to share as a conduit of blessings in my mind's eye.

In the "What about me?" theory of individuality, people become a reservoir for anything and everything. They believe all good things are made for them. They think that they should gather goods to themselves and hoard them. All their life experiences, whether relational or material, are derived and directed toward themselves. They embrace all life has to give them with open arms. Unfortunately the flow of blessings stops there with them. When this happens, people become stagnant. All the good things in life are bottled up and wasted. How many things does one person need?

When our needs are met, the "things" or the "relationships" that we have become desires instead of needs. There is nothing wrong with having the things that we desire. I believe that blessings should come our way. But I also believe that as those blessings flow to us, we should then let them flow through us. It is the "What about me?" attitude that hoards and holds onto things. It is self-directed and self-concerned. There is caring going on, but it is about "self." Take a look at yourself and evaluate where you stand on these issues. It is time to grow past this immature stage and begin to mature relationally. We call this having a social conscience.

Developing a social conscience is not as difficult as you might think. Actually it is already inside you. It is human nature to develop social contacts and relationships. It is an innate desire among all people. The challenge comes when we draw the lines of responsibility and accountability. These conflicts stem way back in time. Do you remember the statement, "I'm not my brother's keeper"?

The guidelines and parameters of relational responsibility are fluid. They do change with societies and create ethical dilemmas at times. In my lifetime and life experience, ethical theories and decision-making guidelines are representative of a Western European and Judeo-Christian viewpoint. There are three basic decision-making models that most people base their reactions on (10).

The "goal-based model" has its focus on the overall good of an individual or a social group. Decisions are based on providing the best outcome for the greatest good of the majority. The second model used is the "duty-based model." This model takes into consideration the outcome, but also considers other circumstances as well to determine a course of action. This model incorporates each situation into the decision-making process.

The third is the "human rights–based model." The decisions we make under this model are based on the fact that every person has some basic rights. The biggest and most important is the right to self-determination in all areas. The decisions made under this model are made by the individual. Again the focus is on each independent "self."

Each of these decision-making models has a place and a function. Their true value is in their ethical outcome. It is important for each of us to be aware of the ethical basis we are using to make our decisions and basing our ethical theories on. I personally believe that there are many decisions being made out of a lack of knowledge or a lack of awareness or reasoning. The news media and TV programming we watch daily direct our thinking about every aspect of life that we may encounter. Will we simply embrace these ethical choices as social norms without thinking about their implications? Only time will tell.

To have an effective social conscience is to consider others and then to do something about what you see. An active dialogue is imperative. No action should be taken on the behalf of anyone without their input. Communication is essential.

But again, we are discussing taking action. Caring is an action work. We need to do something!

We derive the word "beneficence" from a social conscience of caring. Beneficence describes the action of making decisions that result in the greatest good for others. These are decisions that cause the least harm to others. As you see, the focus is on the other person, not on your "self." Our thinking needs to be more socially balanced. The focus needs to be for the good of others, but not excluding the good of "self."

This kind of thinking is a balancing act of the wills. At times it becomes an ethical dilemma. Believing the theory that we are blessed so that we can be a blessing to others is a balanced thought process. We need to be a conduit instead of a reservoir. A reservoir continually receives unto itself, a conduit flows freely. The subject could be tangible items or social experiences. Either way, good things come to us so they can flow through us. That is the essence of caring. All of us as individuals possess the power to care. We have the power to make a difference in the lives of others around us. This power needs to be utilized, not relinquished. The benefits of caring come from the experience of doing good.

The power of caring comes as we give to others. It is in that process of giving that we will receive blessings in return. There are benefits for us personally as well as corporately. The act of caring is powerful. It has the ability to touch and change lives. Every person has that power within themselves. It is a power that just needs to be recognized and exercised.

Chapter 4

The Power To Do Good

The act of caring is a powerful tool that each individual has at their disposal. It is within each one of us. We have that innate drive within us to be socially connected to those around us. It is in that connectedness that caring flows. It is when these acts of caring begin to flow that we can see the tangible effects of our caring hearts. Acts of caring translate into what we call "service."

The desire to do good is within all of us. The term "good" has many facets, but it comes down to being agreeable and wholesome. For a simple girl from the Midwest, it means being sociable with others—simple politeness if you will. All of our actions should be flavored with consideration for those around us on a day-to-day basis. We need to put aside that reservoir mentality of always seeking to get things to collect and store up for ourselves. The conduit mentality of being a constant source of blessings that is open to receiving as well as open to flowing outward.

That natural consideration for others we have contact with is what service is birthed out of. When we have thoughtful and sympathetic regard for others, we will become aware of the needs around us. The next step would be to act on that perceived need. Service is acting on the needs that we observe. We can then contribute to others' welfare by acting on those perceived needs. This is the act of caring. The power to do good is within every one of us. It is a power that lies dormant in many people because of lackadaisical attitudes or perhaps just a lack of knowledge. It is time for our hearts to wake up and accept the challenge.

The Benefits of Caring

There is a cost to caring; we have already seen that. That cost is dependent on each situation and it can vary greatly. The good news is that the benefits outweigh the cost. Not only do our caring acts benefit those recipients of our attention, but those caring acts also benefit us personally. The acts of caring can also have an impact on the world around us. The benefits of caring are far-reaching and have a lasting impact.

Of course the benefits to those you help are obvious. The greater the need, the greater the impact. If you have ever been involved in a situation where you were the person in need, you know that it can be a spirit-crushing experience. Having someone reach out with compassion to help your situation is a heart-moving experience. Not only does it touch your heart, but it also moves your spirit and your life is changed from that moment on.

These needs for compassion can be recognized if you are tuned in to caring. These acts are especially apparent during times of great disaster. Sometimes we call these disasters "acts of God." I prefer to call them "acts of nature," but nonetheless they are devastating. Living in the aftermath of a tornado, hurricane, or earthquake is difficult to comprehend unless you have experienced it. It is during these times that our hearts open and we pour out our compassionate caring. It is common to give of our pocketbooks as well as our time and talents. These times are an exception to the rule. Thankfully these situations do not happen too often.

Anyone you speak to who has given of themselves in such a situation will relay to you the great inner satisfaction that comes from helping others and doing "good" for someone else. If it is such a wonderful experience, then why do we only do it on a limited, one-time basis? Why do we not do these good works on a regular basis?

One reason is our vulnerability to the abuse of being taken advantage of. Unfortunately that might happen. There are those out in the world whose focus is on themselves. They lie and use others fraudulently for their own gain. Shame on them.

How should that affect our giving and caring?

I implore you not to let that affect your actions. The act of caring comes from a willing heart that wants to touch someone else's life. Your acts of caring are effective. The responsibility then lies on the receiver of your good works to utilize them appropriately. Your blessings will continue to flow even if you were fraudulently used.

> *Do not stop being a blessing because of those few people that abuse your good nature.*

I have heard people say, "Boy, was I a dope to trust them." Reaching out to others does involve risks. There may be risks of misappropriation of your caring acts. You do not need to take responsibility for those wrongful deeds. Those people that misuse your good deeds will be held accountable and responsible for their actions. Our focus should be to continue to give from a willing heart. Be that conduit of blessings, constantly flowing and blessing others. Do not stop being a blessing because of those few people that abuse your good nature. There are so many more that are truly blessed by our service and are in need of our gestures of goodwill.

In the aftermath of Hurricane Katrina in 2005, there were stories of abuse and misappropriation of goods and services. I saw a television program focusing on people that were affected by such abuse. There was a husband and wife couple who had been victimized. Their home was offered for use by Katrina victims free of charge for the use of hurricane relief. A family was moved in and they used and abused the home. Later it was discovered that this family were not even victims of the hurricane. They were not victims at all. This young couple continued the interview by describing the situation. But it was apparent that their loving and caring heart triumphed even through this experience. When they were asked the question, "Would you do it again?" their overwhelming response was "yes." They did not take responsibility for the receiving, but their responsibility was in the giving.

It is important that we learn from our experiences. Once you become aware of an abusive situation, then you need to learn from your mistakes. Remove yourself from its influence. It is not necessary to allow abuses to continue. Remember you must balance care of others and care of yourself.

We must remember to be the conduit for blessings. Blessings come to us, so they can flow through us. Do not let bitterness and unforgiveness block the flow. It is the person with a self-centered attitude that gives to others to see what they can get in return. That is a selfish giver. It is important to learn to freely give. To give freely is to be an open conduit of caring. This attitude of caring will give to others without the worry of the consequences and your reward will come to you on its own.

The principle of reciprocity will work in our lives if we simply focus on our part: to care about others. The principle of reciprocity works in harmony with a giving heart. The principle is a force of nature. It is based on the fact that what is given away will be given back to you. What you give will be given back to you, whether good or bad. The golden rule exists because of this principle. What you give is going to be returned to you. It may be good, it may be bad, but it will come back your way.

If you give with a good intention from your heart, good things will return to you. Do not be concerned with the responsibility of the recipient. Do not let their bad intentions clog up the flow of your caring. As you let the conduit of caring flow through, the principle of reciprocity will return the blessings to you. This is a great benefit of a caring heart. This benefit is not only with tangible blessings, but there are also spiritual blessings that will come your way. So do not let the blessings that belong to you be stolen from you by others. They will be held accountable for their actions.

Chapter 5
Confusing Concepts

Goodness is a concept that everyone is taught from childhood. Goodness means that we will have acceptable behaviors toward others. As we grow up it is only natural to want to do good. That which is good, is characterized by being beneficial in its effects on others. Good things are morally honorable things that have a positive effect on others' lives. The concept of goodness translates into actions toward others around us. It is our destiny to touch the world around us one person at a time. That action then becomes interaction. When people begin to interact, priorities begin to rise and sparks begin to fly. At this point we begin to wonder why we wanted to help anyway! It is at this point that we need to be assured of our intentions and our objectives in our interactions with others. We need to be sure that the concepts of our social interactions do not get jumbled in our minds and then become misunderstood concepts.

Years ago when my sister's children were small, my niece had a phrase she used a lot to express her dislike of any given situation. When life was not going according to her plan, she would use this particular phrase, "That's not fair to me!" It became a long-standing joke in our family. Whenever issues arose that we did not like, we would quote her in a facetious way. It became a joke to our family, but the reality of her young attitude was so very true. This may have been the groaning of a small child, but it is a real reflection of the nature of all people. We have that "I, me, mine" mentality. That "What about me?" expression of importance. We naturally have a self-centered focus that never completely goes away. All our decisions, no matter how noble they may be, reflect back upon the impact that will be felt upon "us." We wonder, "Will our decisions help or have a positive influence on our own lives?" Will these decisions have a negative impact on our own lives? Perhaps it may not affect our lives in any way. We surely don't like being left out of the loop either. No matter what our motivations are, we always focus on how it will impact our own lives.

That self-centered focus also affects the perception of some of the concepts that we live by as well as our responses we use in dealing with others. I want to look at a couple concepts that get confused in the fog of self-centered thinking. As we understand these concepts we can know that our good behaviors are actually helping others.

Consideration versus Caring

In the process of social interactions, it is vitally important that we consider others. The first step in the process of caring is to open our hearts and then make a connection with others. We must offer our attention and listen to others before we can have consideration of any kind. Listening skills do not always come naturally. There are some basic skills to becoming a good listener. Let's review the basics.

To be an effective listener your attention must be focused on the speaker. Active listening takes effort and thought. There are noises around us every day and we become very experienced at screening out those sounds that are not essential to the moment. If you have ever raised small children you know exactly what I mean. We call this selective listening. To be an effective listener, effort must be put into the listening process. It takes deliberate thought.

Not only do we need to "hear" what others are saying, but we also need to appreciate their situation. This is the second stage of actively listening. We must be open to listen to their point of view. Let them express their purpose and reasoning for their ideas. At this point we must use our process of consideration for their situation. The process of consideration takes careful and continuous thought. It is not making a quick synopsis of the situation and making snap judgments with quick answers.

Having consideration means that we will give any given issue some deliberate thought. At this point we need to take everything into account and with thoughtful and sympathetic regard, evaluate the situation. In other words, we need to "think about" the issue at hand. That's not always as easy as it seems. In today's society we want quick answers and we want our problems solved immediately. Consideration does not happen quickly. We need to slow down and give important issues the time they are due.

When these two steps to active listening are followed, we can then begin to respond instead of reacting without thought. This will assure that our response is appropriate for the situation. The response that we have when meeting needs must meet "others'" needs and not particularly our own. We need to know their expectations and their priorities. It is impossible to respond appropriately unless we had been an active listener.

Consideration is the thought process of caring. It is an important starting point. Unfortunately it sometimes becomes the end phase of a heart that wants to care. How many times do you remember hearing the phrase, "I'll be thinking about you"? Or maybe you remember thinking, That's a shame, or I am sorry for you. Your heart is in the right place but unfortunately you stop short. You feel bad for them but you do not follow through and actually help them. Caring takes action.

> *A compassionate heart is the starting point to facilitate the act of caring.*

It is when we respond to our considerations of others that the action of caring begins. Caring will facilitate that their needs are getting met. Caring also will empower problem solving. Creative and new ideas will begin to surface as we help one another and support each other. Caring behavior helps others help themselves. It is not our responsibility to carry the world on our shoulders. When we begin to link together with others in teamwork we will begin to solve problems. We create change in the world around us. No one can stand alone and be effective. We must partner with others. When we mix our compassionate heart with deliberate action, then we have a true and real heart to care. It takes action, however; contemplation alone is ineffective. A compassionate heart is the starting point to facilitate the act of caring.

Sympathy versus Empathy

Whenever we are dealing in the social arena we need to be cognizant of others' feelings. In developing our consideration for others, we need to actively listen to their situations. Without actively listening, we will not really hear what they are saying to us. Oftentimes as we listen to others' troubles we become sympathetic to their plight.

Because of our genuine compassion for others we become sensitive to their situation as well as their emotions. It is important that we remain empathetic with them to gain a clear picture of their situation during the listening process.

The lines between sympathy and empathy are easily crossed and blurred by most people. The difference is in the personal perspective of the situation. When we talk about empathy we are discussing the ability to accurately perceive other persons' feelings. We will then be able to understand the message they are trying to share with us. It is important that we do not mix in our own expression of feelings into the other person's situation. We must always maintain our separate identity. The focus is on the other person, not ourselves.

A sympathetic response to a situation will draw us into the other person's situation and the reflection and consideration become our own. We make their event our own personal event. The listener's thoughts and feelings begin to blend with the one who needs consideration. Sympathy will express compassion for the situation but the focus becomes a mutually shared focus. The focus becomes about our personal selves. Again, as I have said before, it is not about you. That "I, me, mine" mentality begins to rise.

Here is a simple example that will display the difference and help you understand the subtle way sympathy sneaks into our dealings with others. Say that a friend tells you that their loved one has been diagnosed with a terminal illness. Then your friend begins to cry. To respond in an empathetic way you might say, "I know how you feel. I had a loved one diagnosed just last year with a similar problem. It caused me to have a lot of mixed emotions. What feelings are you wrestling with now?" You then can listen to their thoughts and feelings.

On the other hand, if I were to respond in a sympathetic way, the conversation might sound like this: "I know how you feel. How upsetting this must be for you. I went through a similar experience last year. It was a horrible experience for me. I was so depressed." You then continue to talk about your situation, correlating your life with your friend's. At this point your focus becomes yourself. I have to gently say this again, "It is not about you!" The focus needs to remain on helping others. A caring heart flows outward; it is not a reservoir to constantly be receiving to itself. If you have previously learned or seem to always practice a sympathetic response, do not feel condemned. It is a common response that people do use. Just remember, "It's not about you!" You need to focus on others and not on yourself. Just learn and grow. Our mistakes can become a springboard to growth if we recognize them. Be open to change. Your life will blossom around you and you will experience personal growth when you remain open to opportunities to learn.

Entitlement versus Responsibility

It is surprising that most people have an inaccurate understanding of the concept of entitlement. To understand entitlement we need to realize that there are two realms of entitlement. There is a physical understanding of entitlement and there is also an emotional response to it.

When the physical realm of entitlement is discussed, it encompasses each of us as an individual. This means that we are entitled or qualified to receive something specific. At times entitlement has a connotation that one has a legal right to something. When we talk about out "rights," our understanding tells us that we have a just claim to something. We have power or privilege that we are justly entitled to. In America, there are some "inalienable rights" that every person is due. A great example would be personal autonomy. Every person should have the right to make personal choices, as long as these choices do not have a negative impact on anyone else. Every interaction of a social being should be cognizant of how it impacts others around them. In the social context, when society allows "bestowed rights" as a whole, the right is a benefit or a privilege. An example in America would be the right to vote. Any legal citizen of particular age has the "right" to vote. It is a privilege that everyone should take advantage of.

In our country we embrace these rights as

entitlements. These rights are things that belong to us as individuals. We can legally lay claim to certain things. We are entitled to them. This fact is true when we look at the physical aspects of entitlement in everyday life. Unfortunately there is an unbalanced view when we begin to think about our emotional response to our ideas about entitlement. When our attitudes reflect a spirit of entitlement it creates people who keep asking, "What else is going to be done for me? I deserve it."

Again, that pervasive self-serving attitude is rising up its ugly head again. I can hear those refrains of phrases sing out in my brain, "What about me?" and "That's not fair to me." It is a natural human response to place "self" at the center of our universe. But just because it is a natural response does not mean it is the best response. It is a shame, but this is our emotional response to the legal entitlements that are around us every day. Entitlement is the name given to an attitude or a way of thinking about our opportunities in life. The attitude of entitlement that people begin to embrace creates people who keep asking, "What else?" We want to know what else is going to be done for us or what else is going to be given to us. Some common phrases heard today are "You are worth it" and "You deserve it." This mentality makes it okay to have self-centered thinking and self-centered actions.

If you take an honest look at our society

today, the attitude of entitlement is not only on a personal level but also on a business level and on a governmental level. The attitude is centered on self, constantly looking for more. This is the point where our rights turn into license. License is the freedom to use rights with irresponsibility. People do not want to take personal responsibility for themselves or what they do. They want others to carry that burden.

Personal responsibility is a hard pill to swallow. Especially if you have been led to believe that others are responsible for you. We have a generation of people who shrink away or even refuse to accept personal responsibility for their actions or for their beliefs. One thought that permeates mentalities is that there are no absolutes. Whatever you want to do or want to think is your business. There is absolute acceptance that there are no absolutes. This attitude is based on self-preservation and self-acceptance no matter what we do or think. These attitudes are based on the love of "self."

To have an effective caring attitude and walk in life, that attitude of entitlement needs to be balanced with a responsible spirit of service. Every person needs to embrace responsibility; for their actions as well as for their beliefs. It is not okay to have a negative impact on others' lives, even if it is a positive event in our own lives. This is when we need to balance our judgments and our intentions. The scale we use to balance these things in our lives is our caring attitudes and our caring actions. We should remember that we are not reservoirs to always take things in, but we should be conduits for things to flow through us. Our focus should be "What can I do to help others?" not "What can be done for me?" This caring attitude will shift the personal responsibility onto us

If you find yourself in a place of need, you may be on the receiving end of a charitable act. Charity is compassionate caring at work. It is the expression of love and caring as it flows from one person to another. It is an attitude of helping and giving. We then see a thankful response from the one who is on the receiving end of caring. Entitlement, on the other hand, is an attitude of expectation without any responsibility of thankfulness or reciprocity.

> *When we embrace entitlement we actively lay down our ability to control our decisions and actions.*

The honest truth of a spirit of entitlement is that it will set us up to be dependent on others. When we embrace entitlement we actively lay down our ability to control our decisions and actions. We become so self-centered and our focus is so totally directed toward what others will do for us, that we lose the ability to act on our own volition and we lay down self-accountability. Entitlement slowly sneaks up on us and quietly works its way into our lives. We are encompassed by it without even the slightest awareness of its existence.

How can we then balance this spirit of entitlement when we are in an actual place of need ourselves? We need to be sure that we always maintain a responsible and active spirit of service. Having one area of need in our lives does not make us completely unable to reach out and help others in their situations of need. We should always be looking for an outlet to help others. Our conduit of blessings must always remain open and flowing.

It is important that we are always giving deliberate consideration to how we can do good for others around us. Always be on the lookout for ways to do good for others and to be a blessing to those around you. Deliberate consideration is to give actual effort to your thoughts. Look for opportunities to do good. These thought processes are simply expressed as having moral excellence. We call it having good personal character.

To have personal character means to "know the good," "love the good," and to "do good." To know the good is to be able to discern the distinction between good and bad. Each person will develop the ability to make wise choices as they grow and mature. Sometimes we learn by listening to others for guidance. Sometimes we learn by experience and it may be by our own mistakes. But that is what life does for us: we grow with all our experiences. We learn responsibility and the importance of commitments.

A sign of maturity is the development of love for the good. This happens when we acquire moral feelings and moral emotions. Not only is the knowledge of good in our mind, but it becomes a part of our heart and our desires. This will help us to be able to empathize with others. We will be able to develop the ability to respect and have compassion for others, aside from what they do for us or despite their situations.

When we know the good and love the good then we will naturally do good. We will make the right choices for ourselves and those that we care about. It all revolves around personal responsibility. That involves taking action in our own lives and not subverting the power of our lives to someone else.

It only takes a couple of steps to achieve personal character in our lives and the ability to take personal responsibility for ourselves. The first step is to have self-control of our personal desires. Again I have to say, "It is not all about you." I am not saying that we should neglect our own needs. Not at all. But it must be balanced with the needs of others around us. If we are conduits, then as our needs are met, we can let good things flow through us. We can then reach out and touch others.

The second step is to be sure that we always remember to have regard for others. Keep the focus on others. Keep your eyes off yourself. Do not focus on your own problems. Of course, we all have troubles, but the key point is not to focus on them. Anything that we put under a microscope appears larger than it really is. Keeping a good perspective on life can happen only when we see the big picture and do not focus on the small segment of our lives.

Another avenue to personal growth is to seek guidance from other people that we trust. It might be parents or other family members. Some other resources are friends, teachers, or business mentors. Find people of good character and look to them for direction and guidance. They will prove to be a great source of growth and support for your life.

As we begin to grow and mature we will realize that it is necessary to have a specific set of ideals to base decisions on. It does not work too well when decisions are indiscriminately made without some basis of truth. Recognize that set of ideals and base your decisions on them. Then great decisions and choices will be made. This will have a positive impact on the world around us and we will be confident about the choices we make. It will not scare us to take personal responsibility when we are deliberate about our choices, when our decisions are based on truth. So what then is truth?

Truth is the reality lying at the base of any matter. It is an absolute force that does not change. When you make choices that are based on true facts then you know your decisions will be substantiated.

An example of truth would be the fact that the

earth rotates around the sun in our solar system. Therefore I know that every morning the sun will rise. That is truth! I can know that no matter what I face today, tomorrow will bring a new day. I can make decisions and make plans based on that truth and it will facilitate my success.

Making decisions without having a basis of truth is creating wishes without substance. Your plans have less of a chance to succeed and time will show those decisions to be weak ones. There is a life lesson that I have learned and it is this—when the dust settles the truth will stand. It does not matter how much chaos is surrounding our lives, you just need to stand quietly and know that the things built on truth will remain. Those things based on lies and deceit will show themselves to fail. That is why your decisions and choices need a basis of truth to sustain the test of time. Then those choices will be good and they will have a positive effect in your life and the lives of those around you.

Fate versus Destiny

I have made a statement about myself many times to students contemplating going into the health-care field. It was this: "It was my destiny to care for others." If you knew me in my preschool days you may have seen me in a nurse costume. I would wear my nurse cape and hat. I would carry my medical bag all over the house while I took care of my baby dolls. There was never a question in my mind as to what I wanted to do with my life. I would grow up and be a nurse. It is my destiny to care for others.

Each of us has a destiny that lies ahead as we walk out our lives. The path that we individually walk is different from person to person, though. Our destiny is not our final destination. Our destiny is to reach out and touch the world around us one life at a time. The destiny of our lives is the journey of our lives. We all have many roles that we fulfill in this life. One of those roles for me is that I reach out as a nurse. How do you reach out?

Our destiny is the outcome of the course of events throughout our lives. It is a culmination of all the many choices we make day to day. The important point is this—it is the choices that we make that direct the course of our lives.

Fate, on the other hand, is the outcome of our life that is determined by an outside force or power. It is a life that is put upon us. If I accept fate then I embrace all that happens to me without a chance to change it. I have no choices and I have to live whatever circumstance that comes my way. Fate happens to you; destiny happens through you.

If I live my life believing that fate directs my future then I have no choices to make for my life. Fate removes my responsibility for the outcome of my existence. Then I need not have intention or purpose in making the choices I make. Why make decisions or have visions or dream dreams if it makes no difference? I want my life to be intentional and have direction. I can have dreams and set goals. Then I can resolve to make anything happen that I set my heart to. That is walking out your destiny.

There will be things that may happen to you that you have not planned on. Things will happen that you do not have control over. That is the nature of living life and it is unavoidable. We do have the opportunity to change the course of those things if we choose to do that. Some changes are harder to make than others. Some can be simple and others can be life-changing. If you are a person of free will, then it is also human nature that you would do the things that you choose to do. When we continue to repeat the same destructive behavior, we are making that choice. We must understand that we are responsible for our own actions and behaviors. That old saying, "The devil made me do it," is simply a way of shirking the responsibility of our actions.

Our destiny is determined by the choices that we make. I chose to follow my passion. That choice for me was to attend nursing school. I have been able to do many things within that profession. It is my passion to teach others to have a caring heart and I am able to do that now.

What if I had not followed my heart's desire?

What if I had accepted life as it was? Yes, it takes hard work to get an education. Yes, it takes a lot of dedication to show up to work day after day. But I was following a path that I had chosen. It was the path I wanted to follow.

When you are doing what your heart desires to do, it does not seem like such a monumental task. You have the drive to accomplish your goal because it is your own personal dream. It is what you choose for yourself.

Seek to reach out toward the goals and dreams that are in your heart. Do not accept your life if you are not happy with it. Do not embrace that philosophy of fate without any chance of change. You can have a destiny. Look inside yourself and find your passions. Set some goals and start walking out your life and fulfill your destiny every day.

The destiny of everyone is to reach out and touch the lives around them one person at a time. Each of us has our own special gifts which we have been born with. It is time to use these personal gifts to reach out and to make a difference in the world around you. That will naturally happen when you have a heart to care. You set your course. You choose your destiny. Be that source of healing and helping for others. Take my dare to care and begin to walk in your destiny. Your life will bloom and your outreach toward others will only expand.

Chapter 6

The Consequences Of Not Having A Caring Heart

Caring is an important aspect of our lives. We are social beings and we have a natural inner drive to have positive relationships with others. Societies are built on those relationships and at times societies' survival depends on those relationships.

> When we do not care for one another we will end up destroying one another.

When we do not care for one another we will end up destroying one another. When those relationships are not good and are not effective, there will be an effect on the individuals involved in those interactions. It definitely has an impact when our relationships lack caring. That will usually have a negative impact on all involved.

Caring is not only giving attention to someone else's problems but is also giving ourselves for that other person. Caring is an action word. Simply giving consideration to someone's plight does nothing for them. It is when we step out and actively help that situation that our caring heart is being put into action. This is when a difference can be made in someone else's life. As we let those blessings that come to us begin to flow through us to others, lives can be changed; situations can be altered.

This brings us to the center of the matter. Does it really matter if I do not care? Will there be a real effect if I do not have a caring heart? Actually it matters more than one might think. The effects are widespread. A caring heart has a healing capacity that affects the body, the mind, and the spirit. Not only will it affect those around you but it will also have personal effects for yourself. Caring not only involves doing specific tasks but it encompasses building relationships with others. When I say that I care, it means that what happens to you matters to me. When one does not have a caring heart it simply means that what happens to you does not matter to me. It is this attitude that can have devastating effects on other people's lives.

Expressing a caring heart encompasses many things. It shows that we are displaying our concern. As we begin to reach out to do things for others, we experience a personal connection. The recipient of our caring knows that we have given them our time and attention. That says, "I care." Giving of our time and attention is a personal sacrifice. At this point the recipient of our caring is edified by our experience and their life is enhanced. Yours will be enhanced as well.

The effects of not caring have a negative outcome. When we do not express a caring heart we are taking away from others instead of giving to them. The act of not caring creates rejection. It communicates that the other person is not important. It demonstrates that you are indifferent to their problem. They are not worthy of our time and attention. At this point the recipient of the rejection feels lost and alone. No one has received anything from the experience, not even the person who did not have a caring heart. All parties have lost. They have failed with their communication as well as having failed at their relationship.

It is usually at a time of loss that people experience their greatest sense of need. Loss is an illusive concept and it means different things to different people. Loss is a feeling that is being experienced by a hurting person in a hurtful situation. It is a feeling that we experience when anything falls short of our realistic expectations. Loss is experienced when we are without some specific thing. It can also be experienced when we are deprived of some specific thing. Loss comes when something of value is taken away from us.

Loss can be experienced at any level. I can experience loss when I lose an important piece of jewelry. That is not as devastating as the loss of a loved one to death. Both are still losses. So there are many levels of loss that we may experience in our lives here on earth. These losses can be physical or emotional. How we can effectively deal with these losses is definitely related to our social connections and how other people in our lives respond to us during these times. It is at these times when our relationship with others becomes paramount to our effective coping.

How an individual responds to loss is also related to the intensity of that loss. Grief is the emotional sadness that corresponds to our loss. The greater the loss, the greater the grief. If I lose a piece of jewelry, even if it is of great value to me, it may cause me frustration and I will know the loss within myself. There would be a much deeper sense of sorrow and emotional suffering if my loss was that of a loved one to death. With a great loss I would feel acute sorrow. Make no mistake, grief can be painful.

It is the natural human response to show our grieving in the physical realm. We express our grief by mourning. Mourning encompasses the external signs of our grief. Mourning varies by the intensity of our loss. Mourning is also affected by culture, personal beliefs, and social acceptance. It is in the expression of our grief that we reach out to others for support. Everyone who has a caring heart is vulnerable to the "pain of grief." We hurt because we care. We reach out to relationships with others to get the support and comfort that we need to sustain us in these dark times. It is vital that those around us are available and willing to embrace us and help in that time of need.

There will be times that people will turn to you for support. The first response of anyone would be to shy away from a hurtful situation. Grief is painful. The pain of grief is not an enjoyable experience. The first inclination is for self-preservation. We may choose to be indifferent to their trouble. The situation does not personally affect us so why should we get involved? We feel sorry for them, but it was not my own family, so it is not my business. This behavior reflects a separation that displays that you are not affected so you remain uninvolved. This is called complacency.

The second response would be that of apathy. Apathy simply and boldly states, "I don't care." You display that other people's problems do not matter to you. Their loss belongs to them and you want nothing to do with it. Apathy shows a lack of feeling and emotion for the loss. It shows a lack of interest and indifference. Apathy seems so very cold-hearted. That is a true statement. But complacency as well as apathy does the same thing; that is, nothing. They also have the same result; that is, rejection.

An apathetic heart says, "I do not care." A complacent heart says, "I care about myself." Both attitudes show a lack of caring toward others.

Either way we are focused on our own selves. Both attitudes produce a negative outcome for us as well as the other person

A caring heart says, "You matter to me." If you matter to me, then I will do something for you. I will be available to do whatever it takes to have a positive effect on your dilemma. It could be something simple. It could be something huge. But it starts with having a willing heart and a will to act.

Having a caring heart is a choice. Once we make the choice to care, the next option is to decide what we can actually do. Stepping out and making that decision to act can be a confusing moment. Self-doubt will rise. You will question yourself. Will I do the right thing? Will they really need what I offer? Will my actions be rejected? Here again I have to say it is not about you. That self-focus will begin to rise but you must put other people's needs as your goal.

Just remember to be sure that your decisions are feasible. Look for practical things to do. Be sensitive and willing to help. Once you take the first step then you will have the discernment as to what needs to be done next. Be sure to do what comes naturally for you. Perform things that fit your desires and abilities. Know your limitations. Do not put yourself into a situation that you can not fulfill.

Making practical decisions is easy when you

reflect your natural instincts. The first thing that you can do is make yourself available. Let your friend or loved one know that you are there for them, not only in mind but also in the physical. This is a time when your listening skills are going to be put to the test. Ask them for specific direction. Ask the question, "What can I do for you?" We are uncomfortable with such an open-ended question. This kind of question places us in a vulnerable position. That person may ask of us more than we planned to do. Just remember the old adage, what goes around comes around.

Again remember to focus on practical solutions. Simple things like basic human needs should be met. Everyone needs food, clothing, and shelter. We could go grocery shopping or prepare a meal. We could do the laundry or clean the house. Providing a carpool or watching the kids after school goes a long way. The list could go on and on. These are things that we already do every day. They may also be just the things that you would provide for someone else in their time of need.

The last thing to do is to be sure and "remember." After the initial chaos of any event of loss, there is a letdown phase. Our lives will settle back into their normal routines. This is the time to remember. Keep in touch with that friend. You can make a phone call or send a card or little note. It seems like such a small token, but it says volumes. It says, "You matter to me." It says that you care.

There is no timetable for dealing with loss. Your presence and your caring will provide long-term unconditional support to get your dear friend past their grieving into a new lifestyle. They may need help to establish new routines and new directions in their lives. You can help them into their new independence. Their lives will then be transformed into their new normal. Be sure to let them know you are there to support them no matter how long it takes.

No matter what kind of loss we endure, the healing phase will follow. It is a natural process and a natural longing in every person to move into the healing process. The healing process restores us to soundness. It brings us back around into a state of normal living. Loss may cause our lives to change from the normal state we used to know. The healing process then restores us to a new state of normal. It is the caring heart of those in relationship with us that jump-starts the healing process.

A caring heart has a healing capacity for those experiencing any kind of loss. When the pipeline of caring is open and flowing, our capacity to effect change in others' lives is unlimited. We can restore health to those around us.

The concept of health is usually thought of in the physical realm. It is common that some think of health as the absence of disease. I would suggest that we look at health a different way. Health is a condition of being sound in body, mind, and soul.

It is a general well-being in the midst of life as it unfolds around us. Life is not always perfect. How we accommodate to our life as it unfolds is our measure of health. How we accept life's changes will produce our well-being. Our goal in all our relationships is to empower each other to adapt in every situation. It is our responsibility to provide them with the support they need to achieve health and well-being. We have the power to do that when we care for each other.

> *Our goal in all our relationships is to empower each other to adapt to every situation.*

Our caring provides not only specific tasks to help others, but it also involves the creation of sustained relationships that support those that our lives touch every day. It is the destiny of everyone to touch the world around them, one life at a time. We were put onto this earth for that purpose. When we do not care, it has a negative effect on the world that is within our reach.

There are basic characteristics of a caring heart. First it is a giving of yourself. Remember you must be a conduit for blessings to flow through you. You can not be a reservoir that collects blessings unto yourself. Caring requires giving, reaching out and touching others.

Caring also requires your presence. You must be available, have an open mind to listen, and understand the needs that have arisen. This is simply the process of building a relationship with someone else.

As your relationship builds, you will be able to have empathy for their situation. Trust your intuition. Your intuitive knowing will begin to develop as you express your caring. Then you will be able to support the other's personal integrity. Our ideas and decisions need to be based on what will be the outcome that produces the greatest good for everyone.

All these issues flow from a caring heart. Caring affects others as well as our own personal selves. It is about building relationships that are productive and effective in helping us accommodate to our lives. When we make the choice not to care, we are having a significant impact on others as well as ourselves. It will only unfold with a negative outcome. Simply expressing a caring heart will change the course of those lives around you as well as your own.

Here is a story that is a guided walk through the grieving process. It is a step by step journey for anyone who is struggling with the grieving process. It is a mental exercise that helps the reader to walk through each stage of loss.

A Journey Of Life

They told me I had to come. I was told I needed this time to deal with my loss. I required some "me time". So I find myself here, sitting quietly on the hotel patio. The breeze is softly blowing through my hair. The air is blowing in off the waters edge as I watch the sun set behind the water. The sky is turning a glowing pink shade and for a few minutes I forget.

I find that I soon return my attention to the pain of my reality. I feel all alone. I do not know that alone time is really what I need right now. It only gives me time to consider why. Why me, why now, why won't this darkness lift?

I awaken to the cool moist air misting across my face. It is blowing in across the edge of the beach here on the lake. I can not believe I slept through the night in that rickety chair. More than that, I can not believe that no one noticed I was out here all night. I see the sun beginning to rise and it is peaking out behind the gray clouds. The beach is deserted in this small town in the early hours of the morning. As I try to stretch my cramped muscles, the length of the quiet beach stretches out in front of me and draws me out to it.

As I put on my flip flops, I begin the long trek down the beach. The sand has a golden glow in the early sunrise. I am facing a new day. Perhaps I can conjure up a new outlook. I can feel my feet dredging through the sand with every step. My feet feel so heavy. I see so many rocks mingled with the sand. The rocks are so beautiful with unique shapes, colors and all of them are smoothed by the water. I spend my time picking up myriads of them. I am trying to find the most beautiful ones for keepsakes but I only end up with a handful. Quietly I slip them into my pocket one at a time.

I paid attention to my destination as much as I paid attention to my rock collection.

Suddenly I was approaching a lone lighthouse. The lighthouse was stretching out into the water and it was reaching for the sky. Its red and white frame was standing tall against the backdrop of the clouds. It was alone in the water. It had a familiar feel to me and I felt at home there.

I was drawn toward the long concrete walkway. I noticed the water splashing across the large breakers. It was then that I noticed the gull. The bird was laying on the rocks edge. Its wings were spread out wide. It tried to move, but only slightly. As I came closer I expected it to move—fly away possibly. I expected it to at least try to react to my intrusion. Not so. Its eyes were wide open, staring straight at me but not really seeing anything in front of him.

The bird needed help, but what could I do. A wild bird in distress has no repose. No safe place to go. Its breaths were shallow and few. For what ever reason, its short life was near an end. I understand the sadness of loneliness and I did not want it to die alone. I sat down on a bolder near its resting spot and waited.

I had no other place to be, so time had no influence on my schedule. Contemplating loss is a dreadful pastime. I had refused to accept it, so I denied its existence. Watching the gull was the breaking point. I could no longer block out my loss. The emotions so long subdued began to flow. Denial no longer had a grip on me.

One tear began to well up and then many began to follow till they were flooding across my cheeks and spilling down my neck and chest. Along with the tears were the angry groans. I was angry with life. I was angry at myself. God was also on my hit list. Life had not been fair. What about me? I did not deserve this. This is not the course I had chosen for my life. I wanted things to go my way—my life according to my plans. But my life had changed and I had no say in the matter. I had no control. I tried, but I could not make God listen to reason. My bargaining was ineffective. Why did he not listen and respond? He could have, but he chose not to. Did he not care? Was my life not important enough for him to bother with? For what ever reason, God was silent and very distant. There I was, all alone and the tears continued to flow.

By now the sun was hot and high in the sky. I was drained of every tear that could come out of my swollen and heavy eyes. My chest was tight and I was exhausted. I walked back to the sprawling beach and I sat down on the hot sand. The calm waves began washing over me and I remembered.

Words from somewhere out of the past came tumbling into my head. I do not know where I had heard them before. Could it be from some Sunday school class lesson? It may have been from some well meaning soul who was trying to touch my withdrawn spirit. It was at this moment that I heard the statement in my memory that God collects our tears in a bottle. What a silly thing to remember. Then I saw in my minds eye a pair of large, strong hands. These hands were holding a big cobalt blue bottle glistening in the sunshine. I envisioned this large receptacle filled to the brim, ready to overflow. Then I heard in my heart, "I have collected every tear. I did not loose even one".

I sat quietly embracing my new revelation. Acceptance is such a simple word but such a hard concept. Reality is in front of me, but I do not want to walk that road. To accept this loss means letting go. I do not want to let go. I loved my life the way it was. I want things to remain the same. Denial seems the easier path, but in the end it is the loneliest. I have to move on to what lies ahead of me. Embracing my loss means I have to relinquish the past. That means I must let go. It seems so much like betrayal. Apologetically I have to do this. I will live on, whether I want to or not.

The release of it is so difficult and yet at the same time brings such freedom. It is a refreshing that brings a release and a renewal. The darkness is lifting like the fog off the lake in the morning. Nothing of my life's existence has changed, but I am no longer clouded by my experience. I am no longer held captive by my emotions. I will never lose the past. That will always be a part of my life. But I am now free to experience the new life ahead of me. It can be what ever future I choose it to be.

I began the long walk back along the beach to my hotel. I am not sure of anything except that I am not alone, and I choose to live on,

Psalm 56:8

Chapter 7
Opportunity Is The Open Door

A caring heart involves a daily walk of ministering to others. Everyone has been created to do just that. You can not reach out to yourself; you can only reach out toward others. The extent of your heart's service is based on the extent of the need that we perceive. We need to be cognizant of others' needs around us or we will miss the opportunity to walk out the destiny of our lives each day.

Opportunities are around us all of the time. From a kind word or a supportive smile, to activities and good works that impact the lives of others. The needs are all around. We will never be able to embrace these opportunities if we do not know that they exist. It takes effort to have a focus on things other than ourselves and our own needs. This is a life balance that we all need to attain. That effort begins in the mind and in our thinking processes. We are facing choices in our lives all of the time. The responsibility for these choices lies at our own discretion. Each of us has a measure of

> *Sometimes the circumstances that happen to us can be out of our control, but we are in control of our responses and actions that we take from that moment on.*

control for the lives that we lead. Life does not just happen to us. It is a culmination of actions and reactions to circumstances. Sometimes the circumstances that happen to us can be out of our control, but we are in control of our responses and actions that we take from that moment on.

Our choices need to have purpose and direction. Common sense is a sound, prudent judgment that comes from ordinary men and women like you and me. When we are faced with important decisions we need to give the issue grave thought. We need to be wise, be flexible, and be balanced. However, we need to make purposeful decisions based on clear thinking, not just based on a whim or a fleeting desire. We need to take responsibility for our decisions and choices.

Great opportunities arise in our lives every day. Some will be opportunities for our lives. Some will be opportunities that will affect others. Why do we seemingly miss these opportunities? They are right in front of us all the time but we do not recognize some situations as opportunities to care. Sometimes we recognize the opportunity but we make a conscious decision not to get involved. The reasons for these reactions may vary. It is when you understand your choices that you can change that automatic reaction into a thoughtful response.

I believe the biggest reason that we shrink back and do nothing is a little four-letter word, "fear." I am not talking about the heart-pounding, breath-taking, and freeze-in-your-tracks fear. This social fear that we sense is not so dramatic or as physically taxing as outright fright, but it is enough fear that it will keep you from walking out your destiny each day. This is a fear of self. This self-doubt and fear will cause you to cower and not step out and embrace the opportunities that are right in front of you and within your reach.

The first self-imposed fear that comes to mind is that of the fear of failure. There are many opportunities that are set before us that are missed because most people do not want to attempt something that they might fail at. There is no proof of failure, but there is no proof that they will not fail. It is in our human nature to stop short, protect ourselves, and do nothing because of this fear of failure. This way we protect ourselves from being left vulnerable to others' accusations.

If we have an understanding that failure will come into our lives at some time, then the fear of failure will not exert such a mighty hold on each of us. No one ever got ahead in life or was successfully creative without experiencing some sort of failure during that process. It is the successes that are shared with the public, not the mistakes along the way. But be assured, mistakes are made during the process of success. However, it is the persistence of creativity and disregard to self-doubt in the face of failure that changes things. The persistence of great thinkers and leaders is what has shaped the world that we live in today. Do not let self-doubt and fear of failure block your pursuit to embrace any new opportunities to reach out and make a difference. Take hold of your destiny and do not let it go.

There are also times of doubt and fear about what to do because of the fear of making the wrong decision. The fear that a specific action or decision will not lead to the perfect result causes immobilization of action on our part. We choose to do nothing rather than proceed forward. Some people will even predict failure in advance of reaching their goal. In their own minds they put together every problematic scenario of failure and then create their own demise before they actually begin.

The fear to make a decision should not paralyze your efforts to seize the opportunities that are placed in front of you. Go ahead and embrace the circumstances as they unfold. If things do not work out, just move on. Sometimes the outcomes do not meet our own expectations. This does not mean that our venture was a failure. The outcome is not within our control. It is what we put into a situation that is within our control. When the outcomes seem to turn out differently than what our expectation were, we should understand that there are many influences in the lives around us besides just ourselves. Use every experience as an opportunity to learn and to grow.

Another personal fear is past disappointments. Some people allow the disappointments from their past to affect their future decisions and actions. It is only wise to learn from our mistakes. But do not let the fact that you have make mistakes in the past cause you to refrain from moving forward and embracing new opportunities. Past disappointments can be used in a positive way to shape your future. They can help you to make better decisions and wiser choices. Do not allow them to control your future by impeding your ability to move on.

Opportunities are around us every day. We embrace them because we believe that they will have a good chance of advancement for us. They may possibly give us a positive outcome. But there are times when opportunities to express caring arise that do not result in a positive ending for us personally, but seemingly have a positive effect for others. This is a time when anxiety arises within us. That self-preservation attitude rises and we have a fear that if we embrace opportunities to help others then we will ourselves experience a loss. We may get taken advantage of or we may have to experience personal expense for another. This is an opportunity of giving and caring. There is no experience of

> *However, to give of yourself when it does have personal cost is the ultimate expression of caring.*

loss to give a smile or a kind word of support. However, to give of yourself when it does have personal cost is the ultimate expression of caring.

The expression of caring that caries our own personal cost is tough to embrace. Whether it is a loss of a possession or it is a monetary loss, it causes us anxiety. The initial human response is self-preservation. It is only wise to have an understanding that there may be a cost to caring. It is also wise to understand that there are benefits to caring that outweigh the costs. Do not let the fear and anxiety of personal expense become a block to your embracing the opportunities that come your way. Your destiny is to touch the lives around you every day. If you invest in others, then that investment will reap dividends for you in the future.

There will be many opportunities placed before you every day. You will have the option to embrace them or not. It is a choice that we have to make. So our choices need to be purposeful. We need to use good common sense. We need to understand the opportunity before us and understand our circumstances as well as our limitations. Have wisdom in your decision making. Have a balanced view of your circumstances and always be flexible and open to changing occurrences around you.

Think about the choices that you make. Take responsibility for your decisions.

Another excuse for missed opportunities is that of time limitations. "I do not have the time," is an often repeated phrase. Everyone on this earth has the same amount of time. The difference is how we choose to use our time.

When opportunities arise we need to actively pursue them or they will get away. There is an old adage, "Time waits for no one." How true that is. Actively pursuing something requires effort and time. There are many opportunities that get away from us simply because we did not bother to act. Caring is an action word. The thinking process of compassion is not worthwhile without the action of caring. Caring says, "You matter to me." If you matter to me, then I am going to take action. Caring will require some time.

> *The thinking process of compassion is not worthwhile without the action of caring.*

How someone manages their time will determine how effective their time becomes. Each of us has the opportunity to spend our time or waste our time. Our time needs to be managed much like we manage our money. We all know that can be difficult.

How many times have opportunities to care been placed before us and we did not embrace them because it would cost us time? Then after we let the opportunity pass us by, we waste that time on unimportant activities that produce nothing of value for us or anyone else. Our time should be spent on things that have value. Investing our time in the lives of our families and friends is time well spent. You can also invest your time in developing new relationships. Investing your time in others will reap dividends that will return to you. That is what our humanity is all about—relationships.

Be sure to pay attention to all the opportunities that you encounter every day to touch and impact the lives around you. Some opportunities will always be with you. It seems these are the ones we take advantage of and become complacent to. There are some opportunities that only come our way a single time. So, do not let them get away. Pay attention to the opportunities that are set before you. Do not ignore them or take them for granted. We all have a responsibility to do our part. Do not shrink away from opportunities, but embrace them. Be open to opportunities and be an open pipeline for blessings to flow from you to others. Be a conduit, not a reservoir. Have a vision to recognize new opportunities and have the courage to do great things.

Chapter 8
How Do I Begin To Express A Caring Heart?

R eaching out from ourselves to help effect change for others is vitally important in a balanced society. We have this desire placed inside each one of us. The next step would naturally be the action, or the actual walking out of the desire to do good. But how? Where does one begin? How can I do that, you might ask.

These are all common questions we face when trying to decipher these longings within us. These are natural desires. Most probably they have been screaming from inside us for a long time. Unfortunately, time has a way of muffling these longings. The experiences of life alter your steps and directions too. Before you know it, your life is changing. Fear also alters our thinking. Many times we are afraid that things will not turn out the way we planned. We also fear rejection. We wonder if our efforts will not be needed or wanted at all. We need not give way to fear. We do not need to judge our efforts of caring in the light of other people's opinions. Their responses should not hinder our resolve even if our efforts are not embraced wholeheartedly at first. The goal of caring is not self-satisfaction. The goal of caring is to meet the needs of others.

It is important to know what exactly it is that you care about. It is as simple as looking within yourself to find what is written on your heart. Even against the passage of time your heart's desires remain. They may be obscured by life's trials, but they are still there. You need to draw them out and rediscover the passions of your heart.

What do you yearn to see happen in the world around you? Are there issues that touch your heart and stir up an emotional response from deep within you? Do you long to see the world a better place? Look to these issues because you already have a heart crying for these things.

Are there issues that make you angry with the mere discussion of them? What things bring you to tears as you listen to dialogues or watch TV programming? Issues surround us every day. Sometimes we see so much need that we have become calloused and our hearts have become hardened. Sometimes the needs seem so great we do not know where to begin.

We only need to look to our hearts to discover those hidden passions. Then we can begin to reach

> *Your destiny is to touch the world around you today.*

out and care for others. Begin where you are. Recover lost dreams that have pricked your heart in days past but have faded with time. Are there any passions that seem to have disappeared as other life experiences crowded them out? New visions will be birthed within you as you begin this inward search. They will be a combination of old dreams and new life experiences. Start where you are today. Your destiny is to touch the world around you today. Then look to find ways of reaching out and touching the lives of those people close to you.

The more you begin to care, the further your grasp will reach. Opportunities will begin to open up before you. Remember to be a conduit and not a reservoir. Be open to letting the blessings constantly flow through you. And flow they will!

I have a simple exercise that I encourage people to take. It will help you begin your focus and will bring some direction for you. There are three simple questions. I challenge you to take a look into your heart. The answers will open up your heart's desires for you and point you in the right direction. I encourage putting your answers in writing so that you can reflect on them at different times.

Cheryl's Caring Exercise

1. **What does it mean to care?**

2. **What do I care about?**
3. **What am I doing about it?**

The needs of the world are vast. They are too numerous for any one person or even one group of people to meet. That is the glorious reason that each of us can reach out and minister to those issues that touch our hearts. There are a great many needs. Each of us must do our part.

Begin to think about the things that move you. What age group of people are you drawn to—children, young adults, or the elderly? Some people are interested in serving the infirm; others prefer those that are healthy. There is great need in the community of the underserved. You may not have a passion for people as much as environmental issues. All issues are important and affect those around us.

Once you recognize the issues that your heart is passionate about, then you need to act upon that passion. There are other people in your community that have those same visions to make their world a better place. Now you just have to find those like-minded people and connect with them. Believe me, they are all around you. One practical suggestion is to open up the phone book. Look under charitable organizations and foundations. They are usually listed with a name that reflects their mission. There are also many listings under social service and welfare organizations. If you have a heart for young people, look to youth organizations and centers. Volunteer hotlines are also available. Keep your heart open and be ready when a need arises. Be assured it will arise.

Your local church is also a place to be of service. That is a gathering place for local people within your own community. The commission of every church is to meet the needs of those people within its reach. You might be surprised at the needs of those you see every week. Everyone comes to church with a smile on their face sharing cordial greetings with one another.

Sensitivity and a willing heart will provide the first step in your walking out a caring lifestyle.

There are some that then leave with a broken heart, never having their needs met, let alone letting their needs be known. It is surprising how you can read between the lines of others' conversations when you simply pay attention and really listen. Sensitivity and a willing heart will provide the first step in your walking out a caring lifestyle.

Web sites are also a great resource of information when you are investigating for an organization or group to assist. First decide what your passion is and then begin to search into that cause. There are a lot of faith-based organizations that have as their passion a ministry to help the hurting people around them. Look to them as good resources. They already know the concept of caring and giving.

It is important to be wise about any organization you begin to become involved with. Use wisdom and discretion when choosing which organization to support. There are safeguards to watch for when you begin to look for association with any group. All reputable organizations will give an account of all their business dealings. Do not feel intimidated about asking for proof of their business transactions. They should gladly share that information with you. They should be proud to let you know all the things they have done. If they are not willing to disclose that information I encourage you to be wise. You may need to seek out another organization that is willing to give you the information that you need.

The first step is to reach out and offer your assistance. Ask these associations what they might need from you. A little bit of time goes a long way. I had a personal experience one summer helping at the pregnancy assistance center in my county. I called them and offered to help. Their request of me was to work for small blocks of time to simply man the center and answer the phone. Most of the calls were for directions to the center. It was not a significant contribution but a necessary one. The significance was in the fact that someone was there. When a young woman in need called that number, a real person answered. That said to her that someone cared. The impact of that may never be known.

The time has come to act upon our hearts' cry. Look around you and be sensitive to what you see. You will be surprised at all the needs that you will become aware of. You may even feel the frustration of seeing so much need that you do not know where to begin or which need to meet first. You must keep a balance in everything in your life. Just follow your heart. Do what you can. The more you do, your capacity to give will grow. It is a natural sequence in life.

Everything has a starting point. It is important to go through the thinking process. You first need to recognize the need and then set a goal. Once the goal is set then it is time to set your action into motion. It is time to take the dare to care. Now is the time to begin.

Conclusion

Dare to Care is a practical look into the art of caring. We all want to believe that caring is a part of our very own psyche and is reflected automatically in our everyday life experiences. We believe it is an expression of who we are and a part of our interactions with others. Unfortunately we are not as versed in the art of caring as most of us believe.

Caring says, "You matter to me." Caring creates possibilities for coping because we partner with those we know to discover new directions and provide motivation to grow. We all need to learn new strategies to put into practice so we can function with a caring heart. The personal concern of a caring heart should be an inherent feature in everyone's lives. Caring is essential to productive coping. Coping is the one thing that all humans

> *Caring is relational and it connects each of us to the human race.*

need to survive life as it unfolds around us. Caring is relational and it connects each of us to the human race.

I have spent many years in the nursing field, giving care as well as teaching other health-care workers the art of caregiving. I have come to the understanding that caring is not something that comes naturally and instinctively. It is a concept that needs to be taught. I also have come to recognize the fact that health-care personnel are not the only professionals that need to learn the concepts of caring. I have a passion to teach caring concepts on a personal level as well as a professional level to anyone willing to listen. Dare to Care is a practical look at the concepts of caring and how to practice these concepts in everyday life.

When we engage in relationships on any level, we find that we run into barriers to caring. Dare to Care has given understanding of why people shy away from caring. As we learn about the concepts of caring, we will more easily and willingly embrace a heart of caring for those things that we are passionate about. Then we will seek out ways to express these new attitudes. Dare to Care has given guidance and practical direction to help the reader to reach out and express those passions.

Caring is a concept that everyone who engages in any kind of relationship should understand and put into practice. It is a powerful expression of our connectedness to others in this tough world that we live in. The art of caring is at everyone's disposal if we only dare to care.

Notes

Introduction
    (1) Kristen Swanson, "Fundamentals of Nursing," page 104.

Chapter 1
    (2) Sister Callistra Roy, "Roy Adaptation Model," Appleton and Lang, page 8.

Chapter 2
    (3) Sister Callistra Roy, "Roy Adaptation Model," Appleton and Lang, page 52.

    (4) Sister Callistra Roy, "Roy Adaptation Model," Appleton and Lang, page 52.

    (5) Sister Callistra Roy, "Roy Adaptation Model," Appleton and Lang, page 21.

    (6) Sister Callistra Roy, "Roy Adaptation Model," Appleton and Lang, page 48.

    (7) Sister Callistra Roy, "Roy Adaptation Model," Appleton and Lang, page 48.

Chapter 3
    (8) T. Gamble & M. Gamble, "Contacts, Communicating Interpersonally," Allyn & Bacon, page 103.

    (9) Sister Callistra Roy, "Roy Adaptation Model," Appleton and Lang, page 8.

    (10) E. Arnold & K. Boggs, "Interpersonal Relationships," Saunders, page 49.

About The Author
Cheryl Masson RN., BSN.

Born and raised in the midwest, Cheryl has been working in the nursing profession since 1974. Upon graduation from Missouri Baptist School of Nursing, she dug into the trenches of the hospital setting. Over time she was involved in many facets of the health care profession.

Cheryl spent several years of her nursing profession on the front lines, giving hands-on bedside care in the hospital setting and in the long term care setting. She has also experienced nursing from a management position. She has known the challenges of creating standards for care and instilling a vision for the future.

Cheryl's desire is to educate others concerning the concepts of caring. She has a passion to educate others to become involved in the fulfilling profession of nursing and to help them blossom into great care givers. She also has a desire to improve and facilitate better environments for all the "helps" professions.

Armed with a love for people and a passion for caring, Cheryl's goal is to encourage positive reflections concerning our overall attitudes and views about the relationships we have with those that are in our lives. Her goal is to instill the basic concepts of caring and compassion as a foundational cornerstone. A cornerstone, not only in the profession she loves, but also as a part of the overall perspectives that we hold toward other people in every aspect of our lives.